James

Sarah K. Howley

Flaming Dove

Contents

Welcome

This epistle is generally attributed to James, the brother of Jesus. He was a pillar of the early church in Jerusalem. He was well known and respected in the city for his devotion to Christ. His letter highlights social issues of status and justice.

The epistle of James is noted for its discussion of deeds and faith and challenging those who would call on only one as the foundation of Christian life. James' rallying cry for both works and faith, however, is only a portion of the letter. He cries out for justice to prevail and questions the behavior of the rich and the deference to the rich by members in the church. In closing, he calls for wisdom, faith and endurance in the Christian life.

As modern-day believers, we were likely not instructed in the traditional way of life in Jerusalem or the Scriptures as James and many of his hearers or readers were. As such, there are a great many passages from the Old Testament which could enrich our understanding of Christian life and teachings. This study sets out to highlight some of those passages to deepen our understanding of James' words and instruction for Christians today.

Each session opens with warm-up introductory questions, goes on to a reading from James and questions related to the passage. Then the study goes to the linked Old Testament passages and questions. Each study session ends with considerations for personal application. Additional tips and suggestions on approaching the study for individuals and groups follow.

Suggestions for Study

This study is designed for individual or small group study and is composed of 8 sessions. It is designed to encourage thought and discussion of the scripture, encouraging individuals and groups seeking God to have conversations about the text. For 'You will seek me and find me when you seek me with all your heart,' as Jeremiah 29:13 says.

General Guidelines for Individual Study

1. Open each session with prayer. Ask God to speak through his Word.

2. Respond to the introductory questions to focus on the theme of the session and what Jesus says in the main reading.

3. Read the passage more than once. Using different translations can offer expanded viewpoints on the meaning of the original text. This study uses the New International Version (NIV) as the basis of questions and quotes. However, any version may be used to provide insight and assist in revealing meaning.

4. This study is designed to offer a starting point for discovery of what God has to say to you through his Word. Because the study looks at how the Old Testament is reflected in the epistles, there are observation and interpretation questions about the readings in James and then about the links in the Old Testament, as well as comparisons between the passages. These are followed by application questions for personal and group discussion. Writing your responses will provide clarity and focus your thoughts on the verses.

5. Use a Bible dictionary or other reference books to look up any unfamiliar words, places, or names.

General Guidelines for Group Study

1. Come to sessions prepared. Some groups will choose to read and respond ahead of time then gather and discuss together; others will gather to read and discuss together. Before beginning, agree how you would like to proceed so all are prepared.

2. Be an active participant in the group by sharing your thoughts and responses to the questions. Groups often have members who are of varied maturity in Christ and each perspective should be valued.

3. Listen to each other. Consider the amount of time that is available for all to share and be careful not to dominate the conversation.

4. Be open. As there are various 'right' answers, be open to considering alternate viewpoints and agree to disagree.

5. Maintain confidentiality of the group. For participants to be willing to share and grow, the trust level in the group must be high. Do not share outside the group unless permission is given to do so.

6. Expect God to meet you in the study. His Word is living and active (Heb. 4:12) and he is present when we gather in his name (Matt. 18:20).

Introduction

James is known for being a book filled with practical advice for Christian living. Consider the wisdom you have received in your time as a Christian. What was the best advice you got? What was the worst?

This letter also discusses justice and right behavior of Christians. Name five ways that people can be unfair or unjust in their treatment of others.

Session 1: Trials and Temptations

James 1:1-18

Opening

If there was a fire in your house and all the people were safe, what one thing would you likely grab on your way out the door? What is the significance of that item?

How do you define faithfulness to God? How is his faithfulness toward us different than our faithfulness to him?

James' letter seems to embrace and encourage us in the sufferings and difficulties of life. Rather than lament, James challenged readers to look forward and find joy in all that happened. The trials and temptations that believers experience strengthened the faith of his readers and can do so for us as well.

Read James 1:1-18.

Reading Questions

How does James' description of trials and testing support the idea of God's tests coming out of love and seeking our good rather than seeking our failure?

How could joy come from these trials, according to James? What other rewards of trials did James mention in today's passage?

How must one ask for wisdom?

James contrasted the poor and the rich. Describe the distinctions of each group.

Where does temptation come from and what does it produce? God's gifts (vv.16-18) are contrasted with temptation (vv. 12-16). How are they different?

Old Testament Links

Wisdom, joy and perseverance were mainstays of the Old Testament life. James pulled the concepts from the past, showing readers that life in Christ was much like life with God the Father. These passages enrich the understanding of life in Christ as James described it.

Verse 5 encourages those who need wisdom to ask for it. Read the account from 1 Kings 3:4-15. What can be learned about joy, perseverance and life from Solomon asking for wisdom?

The rich are called to humble themselves in verses 10 and 11. How is that concept expanded or described by these passages: Proverbs 18:11; 23:4-5 and Ecclesiastes 5:10-17?

Application

What trial or testing have you recently faced? Describe the joy, perseverance and life that you have seen through that time.

How might the teachings for the rich help hold your own finances and material gifts loosely? When considering the item you would save from fire, would you trade it for something else now? Why or why not?

Session 2: Listen and Do

James 1:19-27

Opening

The last time you were really angry, how did you respond? Was it immediate or held in; simmering or explosive; active or quiet?

List two of things about yourself that make you a good friend.

The second part of James' opening chapter began with a mouth full of words and emotions on our sleeves, calling out the readers for lack of discipline. The call for consistency in religious life is a refrain throughout the book, but heavily emphasized here - even for today.

Read James 1:19-27.

Reading Questions

In verses 19 to 21, James describes anger in relationship with others and with God. Take a moment to consider what the verses say about relationship with God and with others.

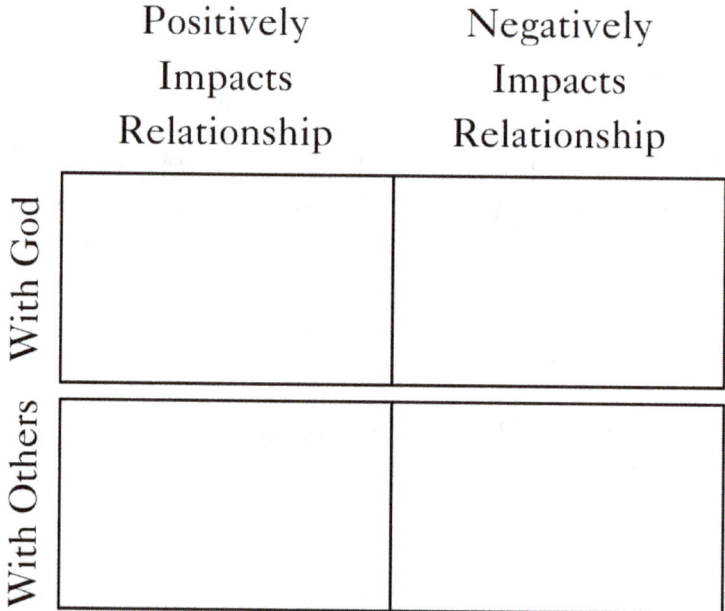

Positive and Negative Impact on Relationship with God and Others

James exhorted the reader to not only listen to the Word but do what it says. Describe what happens with the word if someone merely listens to the Word versus when someone listens and then does what it says to do.

How does the analogy (vv. 23-25) help in understanding what believers are encouraged to do?

Religion is linked to tongues, or the words we say, in verse 26. Why would tongues, or the words we say, be so influential in a religion?

The word "religion" in verses 26 and 27 gives the idea of worship expressed through rituals in the original Greek. What underlying message is James giving in the context of worship?

Old Testament Links

The Bible is also known as the Love Story of all time – the love story in which God pursues his people again and again. He reminds us of his love and all that he has done for us throughout the book. We sometimes miss these reminders from the original language that we are desired in relationship with God. Consider the reminders in the passages below.

The word "face" used in verse 23, "...someone who looks at his face...," includes an adjective in the original Greek, "genesis face." The word has a root which refers to "origins or ancestors". However, it also reminds us of the creation story and how we are made in God's image (Genesis 1:27). How does this change the understanding of the image and remembering who the man is after looking into the reflection of the perfect law?

Deuteronomy 24:19, Isaiah 1:17, and Exodus 22:22-23 express some of God's thoughts toward the widows and orphans. As part of the laws and instructions given in the Old Testament, how are these different from the instruction that James gave?

Application

How good of a listener are you? What specific things or tools can you use to listen more and speak slowly?

Make a note of any acts of worship by the tongue which have come to mind that need reinforcement or reining in.

Session 3: Law that Gives Freedom

James 2:1-13

Opening

The adage, "Don't judge a book by its cover" is often said in regard to snap assessments. When is it acceptable to make judgements about things and people? Is it ever?

Has a snap assessment of a person ever led you astray? How long did it take before recognizing your mistake and changing your mind about that thing or person?

James focused on the difference in status between people who may enter a meeting, but today we may find much more diversity and more opportunity for preferential treatment. The reminder that all are our neighbors, and should be treated as such, challenged the diaspora Jews as it should challenge us today.

Read James 2:1-13.

Reading Questions

James' caution against showing partiality to church members or visitors may look different today. What kinds of external signs may cause someone to sit further away from a churchgoer? And what may cause someone to sit nearer or have a neutral opinion?

James speaks of judging those entering a meeting and those dragged into court. What do these settings have in common?

Often legal proceedings were held in synagogues, similar to local community centers. Does that change the perspective on the admonishment that James gave?

How did James remind the readers of this letter who their neighbor is?

When reading sins such as murder and adultery, it can be easy to distance ourselves from the sin and lawbreaking that James pointed out in verses 10-11. Exchange two more common sins for adultery and murder and rewrite verse 11b here with those sins.

James repeats "law that gives freedom" in 1:25 and 2:12. What kind of law is this that he referred to?

James linked the "law that gives freedom" to mercy in judgement. Draw the connection between the two more explicitly.

Old Testament Links

Justice was an important topic among the laws given in the Old Testament. The ideas that James put forth to treat others without favoritism were a part of the old culture as much as James encouraged it to be part of his own culture. God's justice is tempered with mercy according to James. Ponder how much that reflects the Old Testament laws as you read these passages.

History has shown that Roman judges often favored the rich. Leviticus 19:15 and 18 address justice in the Jewish culture. Read these two verses and Exodus 23:1-9 and discuss the challenges Jews may have faced in Roman courts.

How were judgement and mercy presented in Amos 5:12, Micah 6:8, and Zechariah 7:8-10. Did James agree with the Old Testament prophets? Why or why not?

Application

What does it mean to speak and act as one judged by the law that gives freedom? List some examples of this.

James 2:13 says, "Mercy triumphs over judgement." In the heat of emotion, this is not something that often comes to mind. Consider a situation this week where judgement was quicker than mercy. Discuss alternative responses to that situation.

Session 4: Faith and Deeds

James 2:14-26

Opening

How do you define faith?

Describe how you felt last time someone asked you about your faith or Christianity.

James continued the emphasis on consistency in this passage. The faith and works discussion was perhaps well known even in James' time. His use of examples from the Old Testament, pre-Christ, demonstrated the message consistency for all time –

God wanted the heart of man which included the behaviors that followed the change in heart. He still does today.

Read James 2:14-26.

Reading Questions

Summarize what James said about living by faith.

What kinds of deeds accompany faith, according to James?

Verse 19 argues that even demons believe. How does this idea support James' position that faith must be accompanied by deeds?

James stated that Abraham and Rahab were considered righteous for their deeds. How did giving examples from the Scriptures further James' argument?

Put in your own words James' premise of why faith without deeds is dead.

Old Testament Links

The Old Testament relied on laws to guide the heart into relationship with God. Some of the accounts in the Scriptures, however, demonstrated the individual's heart, or relationship with God, through the works rather than following laws. The same message has been delivered in two ways. Consider how these passages show faith and works of the Old versus the New Testaments.

James addressed his letter to the diaspora of Jews and in verse 19 refers to a traditional Jewish prayer, the Shema. Read the

Shema, found in Deuteronomy 6:4-5, and compare how these verses describe belief in God with that implied by the demons.

Rahab's story is found in the beginning of Joshua. Read verses 2:1-21 and 6:22-25. How did she demonstrate her faith in the account of Jericho?

Application

Is it easier to show your faith in deeds or to declare it? Why is that? List some of examples.

What do you do that shows your faith to others, as James urged believers?

Session 5: Taming the Tongue

James 3:1-12

Opening

Recall the content of the last rumor you heard. How accurate was the information conveyed?

There are many sayings about "words", such as "a picture is worth a thousand words". What old adages, rhymes, or sayings do you know regarding our words?

The number of verses spent on the negative outcomes of our words greatly outweighs the positive in this passage. The power of such a small part of our bodies was important to impart to

James' readers, undergirded with the use of many metaphors about the tongue. Today we find our words more in the public eye than ever, particularly if a picture is worth a thousand words.

Read James 3:1-12.

Reading Questions

Why would James say that those who teach would be held to stricter standards?

What grace did James offer to teachers?

What did James highlight by giving the example of horses with bits and ships with rudders?

James also compared the tongue to fire and to animals. What sense does this evoke as you read verses 5b-8?

The final contrast that James made in this reading showed that nature yields according to its own pattern. Describe how the nature of the tongue is revealed as similar to water and agricultural yield.

Old Testament Links

The damage caused by words and a quick tongue wasn't new in James' time. The pain and suffering from poorly tamed lips equated to death while advice and praise brought life, as they do today.

Proverbs 12:12-23 and 18:20-21 also mention the impacts of the tongue on man. How did James adapt the teachings in Proverbs for his audience?

Psalm 58 echoes the poison of the tongue. What hope does it offer compared to the passage from James?

Application

James implied that no one could tame their tongue. Do you agree with him? Why or why not?

In churches today, we may not "curse human beings", however other sins may be more prevalent. Consider what sins come from the "mouth" and how they may be curbed.

Session 6: Wisdom from God

James 3:13-4:3

Opening

Who is the wisest person you know? How would you describe them and what kinds of things do they do?

Is wisdom linked to faith? Why or why not?

Many have said that wisdom comes with age, yet biblical wisdom is given to any, according to James. This part of James' letter, according to historical and cultural studies, seemed to respond to general wisdom that revolt against the government was acceptable. Describing the wisdom of the world and the wisdom of God contested that thought. James segued from talk of war to the desires of the heart causing strife. The juxtaposition of the big conflict and the small may seem to minimize the desires of man's heart, but James turned it back to God and the heart that he still wants today in his followers.

Read James 3:13-4:3.

Reading Questions

What two kinds of wisdom are described here? What result does each have?

Type
of
Wisdom   Result

How were wisdom and quarrels both tied to motives in this passage?

Old Testament Links

Wisdom was personified as a woman in the book of Proverbs and the wise son is mentioned many times in the same book. When looking for what God finds important, sometimes it jumps off the page in a clear way like this. James returned to the comparison of the world and God, this time in talking of wisdom for all. Today too, God's wisdom is available for all.

Solomon became known for his wisdom after having asked for it from God when he was installed as king of Israel. How was James' wisdom similar or dissimilar to the description found in 1 Kings 4:29-34?

Proverbs 30:8-9 also discuss prayers. How are these contrasted to James' complaint in 4:3?

Application

What good and bad desires battle within you? Consider thoughts, actions, decisions to be made and the struggles that come forth from them.

Take a moment to consider what you may have desired but not yet asked God for. What has kept you from asking? Write out a short prayer about this.

Session 7: Good Neighbors

James 4:4-12

Opening

Who do you think are enemies of God today? What do they do or believe?

What does slander, something said that damage one's reputation, look like? Give at least three examples.

James here held neighbors and being neighborly as a reflection of the state of a believer's relationship with God. God is jealous, in that he wants the person to be wholly his and place that relationship above all others. That primary relationship would then influence all others, in our speech and actions.

Read James 4:4-12.

Reading Questions

People are labelled "adulterous" in verse 4. Define this kind of adultery against God.

Describe the juxtaposition in verses 7 and 8 between God and the devil in relation to the believers' actions.

James spoke indirectly to the readers, beseeching them for a change of heart in verses 9 and 10. What was James asking of the readers?

What is said of slander and judgement in the final verses of this passage. How is involved and in what ways?

Old Testament Links

The posture of the believer was important to James throughout the book. Treating others without favoritism and humbling oneself are emphasized in this passage. It is important to understand the meaning behind the positions that James described, as understood in his time, as language has evolved over the ages. Consider the Bible's meaning of these ideas as you read the following verses.

A number of examples of humbling oneself can be found in the Old Testament. Consider these two passages and the meaning of "humble" behind each example, 2 Chronicles 7:13-16 and Genesis 41:15-36. How are these two definitions of "humble" illustrated in the James passage?

2 Chronicles 15:1-8 illustrates verse 8. How does this short account help in understanding James' point in verses 6-10?

Read Leviticus 19:16-18 which verses 11-12 echo. What is the underlying "do" rather than focusing on the "don't slander"?

Application

James encourages his readers to "submit yourselves, then, to God," (v. 7). What does it mean to live out this submission according to the passage ?

At the time of James' writing, neighbors were those that the readers were dependent upon in many ways. They were the colleagues who had to finish their part of a project so you could, they were the spouse or child or mother who helped to get things done. Neighbors were babysitters and teachers, doctors and friends. Consider what damaging things may have recently been said within your hearing (or from your own tongue). How could you gently turn away this kind of conversation or gently rebuke the speaker (or yourself)?

Session 8: Warning to the Rich

James 4:13–5:6

Opening

At what point does one become "rich"? What is the definition of rich?

What are struggles that the rich face compared to the struggles that the poor face?

This passage seems to be an admonishment for the rich, yet similar accusations could be said of anyone with plans that do not include God, anyone who has not treated others with respect. James seemed to include anyone in his admonishments in this passage, with only a small acknowledgement to do good to others.

Read James 4:13-5:6.

Reading Questions

What is the specific sin that James called out in verse 13? How is that different from the suggestion in verse 15?

How does verse 17 further support James' point about arrogance in the passage from verse 13 to 16?

Describe the condition of the rich and the oppressed. Consider the time concurrent with the writing and describe the future for both parties.

Paraphrase the warning the author gave to the wealthy in this session's reading.

Old Testament Link

The heart of the rich and the heart of the poor is what James was determined to change through his warning. His message intended to stir up the hearers to action for good, based on the attitude of the heart. That message extended to considering the needs and desires of the poor, or the others in our radius of influence.

Many sayings can be found about prudent behavior in the Bible. Read Psalm 39:4-6, Proverbs 6:6-11, and Amos 4:1, 6:1 (optionally read also Proverbs 20:18, 24; 24:27-34; 30:24-25). Describe the attitude of heart that these verses discuss. Discuss how James agreed or disagreed with that attitude.

From James 5:1-6, the passage speaks of what will happen to the rich. There is one thing the rich have done that is explicitly stated in Deuteronomy 24:14-15. Read those two verses and identify what additional information the verses offer. How does that information help explain the issues the poor may have?

Application

Two adults with a household income of $50,000 annually are richer than over 90% of the world population. How do you consider James' warning given this statistic?

What actions or thoughts have led you to feel poor or oppressed? These may be your thoughts and actions or those of others. Given James' points about the riches of God, how can you counter those thoughts or feelings?

Session 9: Communication with God

James 5:7-20

Opening

In what situations do you most often hear promises? How credible, or believable, are the promises?

Describe your habits in communicating with God. What is the frequency and quality of that communication?

The final words in this epistle seem to encourage the readers to persevere with joy in all things. Sufferings, sickness, sin, were addressed with compassion and the mercy of God. The closing seems fitting as it called the readers to remember God in all occasions, good and bad, painful and happy. Prayer was a fine close to the communication with others about God.

Read James 5:7-20.

Reading Questions

What examples of patience were given in the passage (vv. 7-11)? How do they differ from one another?

In verses 13-14, three situations are given. What is the common response to all?

What reasons did James give to confess?

What evidence of power in prayer did James give throughout the verses in this session's passage?

What benefits are listed in turning "a sinner from the error of their way"?

Old Testament Link

The Old Testament was divinely inspired, as the New Testament was. It offers additional information and context to understand ideas that the epistle writers may not have felt was necessary to expand upon. Consider the ideas presented in this passage as the Old Testament writers thought of them as you read these verses.

Deuteronomy 11:13-15 closely aligns with verse 7. As it follows on from the warning in the previous verses, what behavior or attitude might James be encouraging?

Job 1:13-22; 42:10-17 offer a reminder of the suffering that Job underwent. How might this patience or perseverance be different from that in verse 7?

What reason is given for the infirmities in 1 Kings 14:4, 2 Kings 13:14? How does this differ from the implication about illness in verses 15 and 16?

Application

Consider the longest-standing prayer that you have prayed for trouble, praise, sickness or other issues. This may be for someone's healing, salvation or otherwise. How has God responded to those prayers? How has your perspective about these things changed over time?

Given the example of Elijah praying and immediately seeing the result, believers too may expect quick responses to prayers. Describe your experience with prayers for healing.

Conclusion

From finding joy in trials, doing as heard, treating all as our neighbor, taming our tongues and submitting to God's wisdom, passage after passage called the readers to seek the heart that God wanted for each of the readers. James seemed to beg believers to follow God's loving example first and foremost, as the law was an inadequate substitute to explain the heart of God.

Based on James' teachings, how would you describe God's desire for your heart?

What did you learn about God?

What did you learn about yourself?

Do you believe that Jesus is the Messiah, the Son of God and have you received life in his name? If so, describe the qualities of that life.

If this is the first time that you have answered yes to the call of following Jesus, please reach out to a local church or the author to share of your choice and find support for your new life.

To continue your deep dive into "Seeing the Old Testament in the Epistles", pick up 1 & 2 Thessalonians to continue your study. Find it at your nearest retailer by scanning the QR code today.

1&2
Thessalonians

About the Author

Sarah K. Howley is a Bible teacher, passionate about helping believers grow spiritually and take on the character of Christ. She is the founder of InspiritEncourage, an author, speaker, and trained Christian counselor. She has lived in over five countries on four continents and takes her own espresso wherever she goes. Sarah and her husband support initiatives for feeding the hungry and for expanding access to reading.

You can find Sarah on Facebook and Instagram @inspiritencourage. To book Sarah as a speaker at your next event, please contact her through her website. For weekly encouragement and information on her latest releases, sign up for Sarah's newsletter at InspiritEncourage.com.

InspiritEncourage

Also By Sarah K. Howley

Women of the Old Testament Bible Studies
Hope: A Bible Study of Women in Jesus' Lineage
Faith (coming 2025)
Love (coming 2025)

Alive Again Bible Study on Forgiveness
Alive Again: Find Healing in in Forgiveness
Alive Again Bible Study: Find Healing in Forgiveness
Alive Again Forgiveness Prayer Journal

The Son Reveals the Father
I Am: An 8-Session Study of John
Heart: A 12-Session Study of Luke
Word: An 11-Session Study of Matthew
King: An 8-Session Study of Mark

www.ingramcontent.com/pod-product-compliance
Lightning Source LLC
Chambersburg PA
CBHW060141150626
46550CB00015B/2577